Standin' Tall®

with

SERVICE

Music by
Janeen Brady
Script by
Diane Woolley and Janeen Brady

Series Includes

1. Obedience
2. Honesty
3. Forgiveness
4. Work
5. Courage
6. Happiness
7. Gratitude
8. Love
★9. Service
10. Cleanliness
11. Self-Esteem
12. Dependability

Heather, Paul, I need you.

PAUL: Come on, Heather. It's time to eat. I can smell dinner way out here.

Hi, kids.

PAUL: Mom, this looks great. I'll start setting the table.

Thank you, but this dinner is not for us.

★ **What do you mean, it's not for us? Spaghetti is my favorite.**

I know it's your favorite. I hope it's the Miller's favorite, too.

PAUL: The Miller's?

I just heard Mrs. Miller is in the hospital, and I thought we could help their family by taking them a meal. Each of you carry something, and I believe we can make it in one trip.

PAUL: Even the sweet rolls?

Yes, and I've counted them, so no snitching.

★ **But why do they have to eat our dinner?**

I'll try to explain as we go.

♪♪ When Mrs. Miller isn't home because she's feeling bad
And Mr. Miller's all alone and feeling rather sad
And they both need someone who cares to brighten up their day,
What should we do?

Give our dinner away?

Let me explain.

Because a friend in need is a friend, indeed,
Let's be a friend to a friend.
We'll be a friend in deed to a friend in need,
For we may not ever have that chance again.

And think about the winter when the roads are packed with snow
And people are afraid to drive for fear their cars won't go.
Then, sure enough, some travelers get very firmly stuck.
What should we do?

Get Dad to shovel it?

Now you're getting the idea!

(Chorus)

And when somebody's getting old and can't move very fast
And they're afraid to use the stairs with people rushing past,
So they just sit around a lot and look at you and smile,
What should we do?

Stop and visit for a while.

(Chorus)

There's a word for it, you know—service.

MR. MILLER: Mrs. Jones and Heather and Paul! Come in, come in.

How's Susan?

MR. MILLER: She's doing fine. What's this?

PAUL: We brought our din— I mean, some dinner for you.

CHILD: It's spaghetti! I love spaghetti. All Daddy can fix is peanut butter sandwiches.

MR. MILLER: I'm afraid that's about right.

CHILD: Peanut butter for breakfast, peanut butter for lunch.

MR. MILLER: I don't have much imagination. This looks wonderful. Will you join us? There seems to be plenty.

No, you go ahead. Use the leftovers for lunch tomorrow. And please call us if you need anything.

MR. MILLER: Thanks so much. Hey, fella, out of those sweet rolls until you've eaten your dinner.

PAUL: Mom, that was great. Did you see that little boy's face when he saw the spaghetti?

★ **Can we do service again sometime? Please?**

Tomorrow you make a list of everyone you see serving others. Then we'll talk about it some more.

PAUL: Okay.

★ **But I have a question. What are we having for dinner?**

Can't you guess?

★ **ALL: Peanut butter sandwiches!**

♪♪ Because a friend in need is a friend, indeed,
Let's be a friend to a friend.
We'll be a friend in deed to a friend in need,
For we may not ever have that chance again.

PAUL: This is going to be hard. How will we know when people are giving service?

★ **Mom says when you get paid for doing something, it's a job. When you don't get paid, that's service.**

LADY: Wait, children. Here comes a car. Stand on the curb until I say it's safe to cross.

PAUL: Is this your job?

LADY: No, not really. I'm a volunteer.

★ **A volun— what?**

LADY: A volunteer. That's someone who gives service.

★ **Without getting paid for it?**

LADY: Yes! I'm a crosswalks volunteer.

PAUL: You're the first one on our list!

★ **We're writing down all the people we can find who are giving service.**

LADY: That sounds like a fine project. May I help you?

★ **If you'd like.**

LADY: I'd love to.

PAUL: We're going to find so many volunteers.

★ **Here comes Mr. Bronsky. I'll ask him if he's a volunteer. Hello, Mr. Bronsky. We're looking for volunteers. Do you give service?**

MR. BRONSKY: Well, yes. I collect toys for children who don't have much.

★ **And nobody pays you for it?**

MR. BRONSKY. Nope. I used to get paid when I fixed cars, but now I collect toys to help make children happy.

★ **Then we'll put you on our list.**

PAUL: I found another one. Over there! It's our soccer coach. He's a volunteer, for sure.

LADY: And his girl friend is a volunteer at the hospital. I've seen her many times talking to the sick people.

★ **And there's Miss Channing. She comes to school and reads with us one at a time.**

PAUL: I thought it would be hard to find volunteers, but it's not hard at all. There are lots of them.

★ **Everybody helping everybody. Just think of it!**

HOSPITAL AID
TOY REPAIRMAN
SOCC
TEACHER
CROSS WALKS LADY

♪♪ We volunteer, we volunteer (whistle).
We volunteer, we volunteer (whistle).
With a smile we'll lend a helping hand.
When life's a trial, we'll try to understand, and
We volunteer, we volunteer. When things go badly,
We volunteer, we volunteer. We'll serve you gladly.
Any little thing that we can do for you,
We volunteer, we volunteer, we volunteer.

We volunteer, we volunteer (whistle).
We volunteer, we volunteer (whistle).
When you're down and life is bittersweet,
We'll be around to set you on your feet, for
We volunteer, we volunteer. We're here to serve you.
We volunteer, we volunteer. We'll help preserve you.
Any little thing that we can do for you,
We volunteer, we volunteer, we volunteer.

★ **This is a big list.**

PAUL: But I don't think it helps us. What service can we give? We're too little.

★ **We're little, but we can do something. We just have to think of it.**

PAUL: Got any ideas?

★ **I'm still thinking.**

PAUL: I know! I know something we can do.

★ **What?**

PAUL: We have to wait till tomorrow.

★ **Why?**

PAUL: Because tomorrow they're picking up the garbage, and you know old Mrs. Russell. Well, wouldn't it be fun. . . .

PAUL: Come on, Heather, we have to hurry.

★ **It's so early. Nobody's up yet.**

PAUL: That's the idea. We don't want anyone to see us, especially Mrs. Russell.

★ **This is exciting. I was worried we couldn't do any service; we're not very big or strong yet.**

PAUL: We're strong enough. Shh! We're here. Let's get to work.

★ **Paul, this is a heavy garbage can.**

PAUL: I'll carry it. You take the lid—quietly. It's a long way to the street. Did we get it all?

★ **I think so. Here's the lid.**

PAUL: She heard us! She's coming. Run!

MRS. RUSSELL: That you, cat? Here, Kitty! Well, that's odd. I thought I heard something.

PAUL: Whew! She didn't see us.

MRS. RUSSELL: Darn cat, never comes when I call her. If she's in that garbage can again, I'll . . . now, I know I put it here. I always keep it right here. If I start misplacing my garbage can, I'm in big trouble.

★ **Look at her. She's surprised.**

PAUL: She's found the garbage can.

MRS. RUSSELL: Why, bless my soul, someone set it on the curb. Gracious me, I wonder who it was. Nice to know someone cares.

★ **That was a good idea, Paul.**

PAUL: It sure was. Now we can put our names on the volunteer list.

Paul, Heather, I have a surprise for you.

PAUL: A surprise?

★ **What is it?**

Here are two little notebooks. I thought you might like to make a service chart so you can keep a record of each time you serve. Today is Friday. See if you can do something to help someone each day, and next Friday we'll see what you've done.

♪♪ This is going to be neat.
This is going to be fun!
When we walk down the street,
We'll be looking for someone
Who needs a helping hand.

All the friends that we know,
Whether grown-up or small,
Have their troubles, and so
We'll keep watch on them all
And try to understand.

Sometimes they need assistance.
Sometimes they're in distress.
So we'll be there in an instant
To make their burdens less.

This is going to be great!
This is going to be wow!
There's no reason to wait.
Let's get started right now
And lend a helping hand.

We'll be on the alert.
We won't have to be told.
If there's somebody hurt
Or if somebody's old,
We'll try to understand.

Even though we're only kids
And though our muscles are few,
When we think of ways to give,
There's such a lot we can do
If only we learn, if only we learn
To serve, we learn to serve.

PAUL: Friday—my first entry. Today I helped my neighbor carry in his groceries.

★ **I picked up papers that blew down the street.**

PAUL: Saturday—I watched baby Jeffrey while his mom went in the house to answer the phone.

★ **I helped a little neighbor boy find his shoe.**

PAUL: Sunday—I held the door open for some people.

★ **I helped an old lady down the steps and across the street.**

PAUL: Monday—I straightened the books on the library table.

★ **I took a note to the principal's office.**

PAUL: I dried off the car after it was washed.

★ **I visited with Mrs. Baker. She's been sick.**

PAUL: I washed the chalkboards.

★ **I took Mr. Clement his paper.**

I cleaned my room.

★ **I sorted the toys.**

It's Friday, children. Have you kept your service charts?

PAUL: I'll show you.

★ **I filled a whole page.**

Wonderful! I'm proud of you. Now, I'm going to ask you an important question. Think carefully before you answer it. How do you feel toward the people you've served?

PAUL: I think I like them better. I care about them.

★ **I think I love them.**

You've done it! You have discovered the secret of service!

The more we serve, the more we love; the more we love, the more we serve.
Around in a circle we go. La, la, la, la, la, la, la, la.
The more we love, the more we serve; the more we serve, the more we love.
The circle continues to grow. La, la, la, la, la, la, la, la, la, la.

Then we're no longer a house of people.
We're a family, and that feels good.
And we're no longer a group of families;
We've become a neighborhood.
A family first and then a neighborhood.
We're people serving, and it feels so good.

Because we serve, we learn to love; we learn to love because we serve.
Around in a circle we go. La, la, la, la, la, la, la, la.
Because we love, we learn to serve; and when we serve, the cause of love
Can reach out forever, we know. La, la, la, la, la, la, la, la, la, la.

And soon we're not separate neighborhoods,
For we've become a community.
And if we all keep on serving,
What a happy country this will be.
A neighborhood, then a community—
Then what a happy country this will be.

Till all the world will know we care,
Because we serve and love is there.
Around in a circle we go. La, la, la, la, la, la, la, la.
And every life gets better still,
Because we serve and love until
We're all in the circle, we know. La, la, la, la, la, la, la, la, la, la.

'Cause somewhere, someone took the time to care.
The time to share.
To love and serve, to serve and love.
We'll draw a circle round the world of
The love to serve, to serve and to love.

SERVICE
AROUND
THE
WORLD

PAUL: We know all about service, Mom.

You know quite a bit, but not all. There's something missing from your service charts.

★ **What is it?**

Your family. That's where service should begin. Heather, how many times did you serve Paul?

★ **Oh!**

And Paul?

PAUL: But she's my sister. Am I supposed to serve my sister?

Yes, and your mother, because when you serve you learn to . . .

★ **. . . love!**

PAUL: But I already love her.

You'll learn to love her even more. It works in a family, too.

★ **I didn't think about serving you, Paul, but I will now.**

It's strange, isn't it, that we learn to love others by serving them.

★ **Maybe that's why you love us so much, Mom. You're always doing things for us.**

Maybe it is.

We need to do a little bit of service every day.
We need to show each other that we care.
And sometimes those who need us most aren't very far away,
For it's the family's burdens we should share.

So don't forget the fam'ly when you want to serve.
Do for them the nice things they deserve.
And someday when you're all grown up, your thoughts will often stray
To the love we felt when families learned to care.

★ **Mom, somebody shined my shoes! I was getting dressed for school, and my shoes were shining just like new. Look at them, Mom!**

I didn't shine them, and you didn't shine them. Do you think. . . ?

★ **I bet Paul did it.**

We need to do a little bit of service every day.
We need to show each other that we care.
And sometimes those who need us most aren't very far away,
For it's the family's burdens we should share.

So don't forget the fam'ly when you want to serve.
Do for them the nice things they deserve.
And someday when you're all grown up, your thoughts will often stray
To the love we felt when families learned to care.

★ **Do you think he loves me more now, Mom? 'Cause I love him more.**

And it's all because of service.

Service with a capital S—
Sharing a burden and making it less.
Service with a captial E—
Each of us easing another one's needs.

Service with a capital R—
Reaching out to others.
Service with a capital V—
Very aware we're sisters and brothers.

Service with a capital I—
Using initiative when trouble is nigh.
Service with a capital C—
Caring and comforting cheerfully.

Service with a capital E—
Everyone learning to lovingly give
S—E—R—V—I—C—E
Service with a smile.

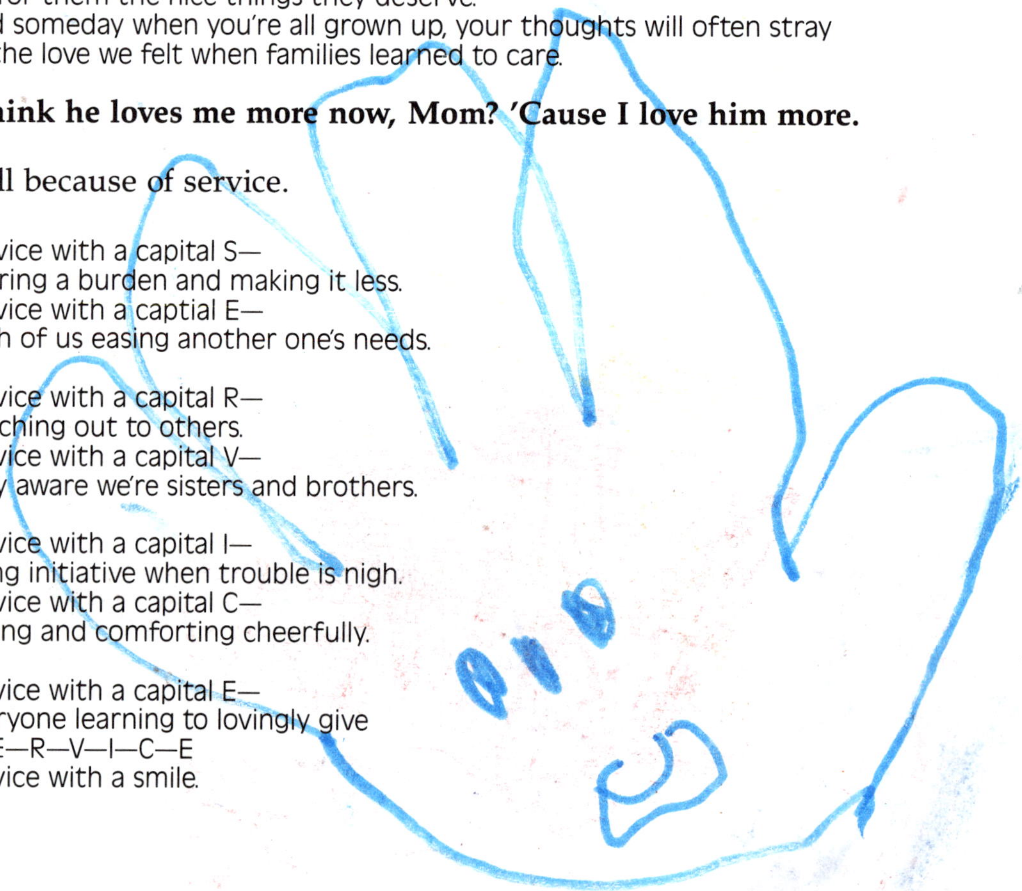

SERVICE
EQUALS
LOVE

Side A of each cassette contains the complete program. **Side B** repeats the same program but leaves out the lines of the main child in the story, giving the listener the chance to read along, saying aloud the missing lines and actually becoming a member of the cast. This fascinating activity helps older children with their reading and provides an excellent opportunity for development in dramatics.

Children can sing along with the songs, color the pictures and participate in still other activities as the story progresses.

Brite

A Product of BRITE MUSIC ENTERPRISES, INC.

Music and Dramatics recorded, engineered and mixed at Bonneville Media Communications.
Illustrations by Grant Wilson / Graphic production by Whipple & Associates.
Music arranged and conducted by Merrill Jenson.